"*I always believed that Israel should be much larger. This book put it all together in an understandable way. I have thought about all of this for years. I have prayed this way already. But this book has put it into a logical form.*"

—TOM NAFZIGER
FOUNDER OF GLOBAL KINGDOM MINISTRIES

"*Excellent. This book points out to the Christian what God gave to the children of Israel. There is a very high percentage of Christians who do not know this! I like the way it was written, both to a believer and a non-believer! This dispels any question about the original land.*"

—RON BAUZA
FOUNDER OF WORD OF HIS GRACE MINISTRIES

"*I believe this book is true. I am in agreement 100 percent. We must pray for this to happen.*"

—JOEL SWALLOW
VICE PRESIDENT OF MORGAN STANLEY IN SARASOTA, FLORIDA
AND PRESIDENT OF SARASOTA FULL GOSPEL BUSINESSMEN CHAPTER

"'*A Nation Born In A Day*' *is calling on intercessory prayer teams worldwide to stand in the gap for the land of Israel that is presently surrounded by spiritual as well as natural enemies. This devotional is designed to keep the intercessory prayer on track.*"

—DR. BILL PETERS

"*This book is a call to faith, a call to prayer and a call to partner with God, however He may lead, in helping to fulfill a promise by the One who is ever faithful and whose Word and promises endure forever.*"

—DR. BERIN GILFILLAN

A NATION BORN IN A DAY

PAUL TOBERTY

CREATION
HOUSE

A Nation Born in a Day by Paul Toberty
Published by Creation House
A Charisma Media Company
600 Rinehart Road
Lake Mary, Florida 32746
www.charismamedia.com

Unless otherwise noted, all Scripture quotations are from Holy Bible, International Version®, NIV®. Copyright ©1973, 1978, 1984, 2011 by Biblica, Inc.™ Used by permission of Zondervan. All rights reserved worldwide.

Scripture quotations marked NKJV are from the New King James Version®. © 1982 by Thomas Nelson, Inc. Used by permission. All rights reserved.

Scripture quotations marked KJV are from the King James Version of the Bible.

Design Director: Justin Evans
Cover design by Nathan Morgan

Visit the author's website: ANationBornInADay.org

Library of Congress Cataloging-in-Publication Data: 2015939487
International Standard Book Number: 978-1-62998-447-6
E-book International Standard Book Number: 978-1-62998-448-3

First edition

15 16 17 18 19—9 8 7 6 5 4 3 2 1
Printed in Canada

TABLE OF CONTENTS

ACKNOWLEDGMENTS

I WOULD LIKE TO acknowledge and thank Dr. Charles Monroe and Joyce Toberty for the ideas and support they have contributed to this book.

INTRODUCTION

M IDDLE EAST STRIFE, increasing global anti-Semitism and dwindling support for Israel among the world's super-powers—these are the headlines of the day. Many solutions are proposed but none seem to work.

There is a solution to the on-going problems in the Middle East but it is hardly ever dreamed of, let alone addressed. It is not even whispered among those in power, though the Bible makes it very clear what the answer is.

That answer has to do with a promise made thousands of years ago to a man who became the father of faith: Abraham.

The promise of land to this man and his descendants, though obscure and seemingly lost in the sands of time, is as valid as today's currency. One day it will be fulfilled in its entirety—I believe very soon.

This book offers keys to understanding God's promises of land to Israel. We must start by being aware that God promised land to Israel, and then we must fervently pray for that promise to be answered.

That is why this book also includes a daily devotional which will help you pray for the peace of Jerusalem and partner with Israel in petitioning the Almighty for the land that rightfully belongs to Israel.

That is our clarion call!

World affairs and our own personal destinies are wrapped up in this Abrahamic "land grant." And so we must pray. This book will help take you along that path. You will first read about the promises that God has granted to Israel. Then you will consider important questions about Israel's destiny and your own. As you read along and pray through this guide you will understand in a deeper way what God has promised Israel—and what He has promised to you personally.

Scripture tells us that we will be blessed if we bless Israel:

> I will make you a great nation; I will bless you
> And make your name great; And you shall be a blessing.
> I will bless those who bless you,
> And I will curse him who curses you; And in you all the
> families of the earth shall be blessed.
> —Genesis 12:2–3 (NKJV)

Let's examine this mysterious and prophetic promise of God to Abraham which will one day redraw the map of the Middle East. Let's stand with Israel and the Israeli people, lifting them up to our heavenly Father. Let's pray that His land grant promise will be fulfilled even in our lifetime! Let's also be inspired by what God has promised to His chosen people and apply those promises to our personal lives as well.

May God speak to you through this book about His everlasting promise to Abraham—and may God inspire you to embrace what it means for your life, too.

—Paul Toberty
Newport Beach
June 2014

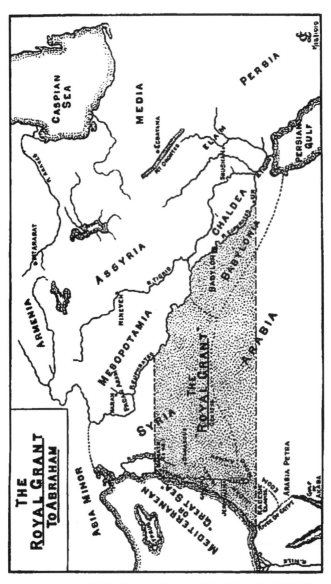

Used with permission of the Rev. Clarence Larkin Estate • PO Box 334, Glenside, PA 19038 USA
• 215-576-5590 • www.larkinestate.com

CHAPTER 1
GOD AND REAL ESTATE

I'M A BUSINESSMAN and a land developer. I have made a living buying and selling land and been on both sides of deals involving tens of millions of dollars. When it comes to land, I know from experience that a contract means everything. A contract gives you possession of a certain parcel of land, the freedom to build on it, to sell it, to develop it. You don't do anything without a contract. Without it, you have no right to the property. This is basic to our system of law and government here in America.

Contracts are also basic to God's Kingdom economy. God owns a lot of land—you may have noticed. He's the original real estate mogul. He created it. It belongs to Him. People divide land, buy it, sell and develop it, but our activity comes and goes. Our earthly lives are temporary as is our ownership of the parcels, properties, and places that make up this planet. Ultimately, it is all His and He can give it to whomever He pleases. The Bible says:

> The earth is the LORD's, and everything in it, the world, and all who live in it.
> —PSALM 24:1

This is such an important principle that Paul repeated it in 1 Corinthians 10:26.

What does God do with all this land? Sometimes He gives it to people. When He does, He stands by His word because His word is His contract.

> God is not a man, that He should lie,
> Nor a son of man, that He should repent.

Has He said, and will He not do?
Or has He spoken, and will He not make it good?

—NUMBERS 23:19 (NKJV)

So when I read Genesis 15, as a real estate owner and landlord of major properties, I see more than a passing promise—I see a contract. This particular contract is between God and Abraham. It has been called God's "land grant" to Abraham. Let's look at it:

> On that day the LORD made a covenant with Abram and said, "To your descendants I give this land, from the Wadi of Egypt to the great river, the Euphrates—the land of the Kenites, Kenizzites, Kadmonites, Hittites, Perizzites, Rephaites, Amorites, Canaanites, Girgashites and Jebusites."
>
> —GENESIS 15:18–21

This may seem like alphabet soup to us now, because the Kenites and all the rest no longer exist. But God was describing something very specific here: the boundaries and territories of a land Abraham's descendants would one day possess. He was painting a picture of a large nation that would one day occupy the fractured map of the Middle East. That territory looks something like the area marked on the map in this book. It includes:

- all of present-day Israel

- all of Lebanon

- two-thirds of Syria, including Damascus

- one-third of Iraq west of the Euphrates River which provides the eastern border (including the city of Ur, the home city of Abraham which today is represented by several mounds or tels just west of the Euphrates)

- a large portion of Jordan, including Amman

- the northern tip of Saudi Arabia which is primarily desert

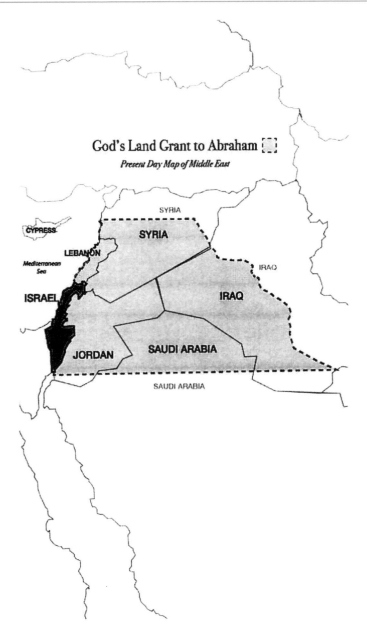

When I began to look at this more carefully, I learned something surprising, perplexing and ultimately inspiring: the boundaries of God's land grant to Abraham have never been fully realized. They were partially realized in the latter days of King David and during the reign of King Solomon, when he ruled as far as the Euphrates River (1 Kings 4:21), but the nation of Israel lived primarily within the more limited boundaries of the land division accomplished by Joshua.

This means that God's land grant to Abraham has yet to be realized, but it will be—perhaps in the very near future.

CHAPTER 2
IS NOW THE TIME?

Have you watched the news on the Middle East lately? There is instability like never before in our lifetimes. Yes, there has been continuous turmoil there for decades, maybe even centuries, but we are in a special time now foretold by the prophets thousands of years ago. Israel was restored as a country less than seven decades ago. That's no time at all, and for those of us who watch closely for the end of the age, it is a major historic and prophetic marker. It means we are speeding toward the final days of this world and about to enter a new era altogether where strife and sin pass away and the Lord reigns forever.

Can I just pause to say a heartfelt "Hallelujah!" May it happen quickly, Lord.

You may have noticed that in recent years the turmoil and instability in the Middle East have ratcheted up. Revolutions are toppling old governments. New orders are forming, new dangers are emerging, and enemies of peace are trying to take advantage of uncertainty. People are being drawn this way and that, not knowing where to put their trust.

What does this mean?

As a businessman I have observed that times of instability are also times of great opportunity. When the stock market swoons, that is often the time to buy. When nobody wants to own land, that's the time to go shopping for properties. Big shifts can happen when things are off kilter, imbalanced, uncertain.

I believe that could be the case in the Middle East. What if events in the realm of politics and international relations took us to a place where a shift suddenly occurred—and the land grant was fulfilled all at once? If you think it can't happen, I point you to the real-life example of Israel which exists and has

existed in defiance of any historical precedent. No other country
has come into existence overnight—ever. Yet Israel did. Israel
shows us that anything is possible with God.

*I believe God wants peace in the Middle East, and that Israel
and the land grant are His means for providing it.*

Have you ever wondered why the Middle East is always con-
sumed with strife? I have an idea and it comes from my experience
in the radio business. I have spent my life not only buying and
selling land but also radio stations. I was an early pioneer in con-
temporary Christian music stations. I owned and operated five stations and provided satellite services to hundreds more. We helped
to launch the careers of singers like Amy Grant and Michael W.
Smith, whose music we played even when it was controversial.

I was also an early supporter of a start-up television station
known as Trinity Broadcasting Network. Maybe you've heard of it.

Owning a radio or television station is a lot like owning property, only you own airwaves instead. To broadcast legally you must
obtain a license from the federal government. A license covers a
certain geographical area and limits the range of your broadcast
so that your station doesn't overlap with someone else's. A license
gives a station "authority" over certain airwaves in that area. This
tells a station how much power it may use, who its audience is and
so forth. Without licensing, the radio and television frequencies
would be jammed up with multiple stations. Nobody could hear
or see anything.

When TBN was a fledgling station, it needed a license to broadcast. For a time they broadcast without one, which could have led to
serious and devastating consequences for that ministry. I was very
concerned they have a license and so I helped them procure one.

When multiple radio or television stations broadcast on the
same frequency there is chaos and disorder. Sometimes I wonder
if the reason there is such chaos and disorder in the Middle East
is because people are occupying a land not designated for them.
It seems possible that they are "broadcasting without a license,"
so to speak. They have intruded onto someone else's property
which God did not give to them. The land itself is against them.

How do we know this might be happening? Just look at the contract. God gave that land to Abraham and his descendants through Isaac. He said to Isaac in Genesis 26:3:

> Stay in this land for a while, and I will be with you and will bless you. For to you and your descendants I will give all these lands and will confirm the oath I swore to your father Abraham.

This promise was passed to Isaac in Genesis 21:12b where God says to Abraham:

> It is through Isaac that your offspring will be reckoned.

Isaac passed the blessing to Jacob in Genesis 27, and God affirmed it to Moses in Exodus 23:31:

> I will establish your borders from the Red Sea to the Mediterranean Sea, and from the desert to the Euphrates River. I will give into your hands the people who live in the land, and you will drive them out before you.

Joshua 1:4 adds:

> Your territory will extend from the desert to Lebanon, and from the great river, the Euphrates—all the Hittite country— to the Mediterranean Sea in the west.

Until Abraham's descendants possess the land granted to them, there will not be peace. I believe and hope that peace will come soon and transform not just the Middle East but the world. Isaiah the prophet gave a moving prediction of the restoration of Israel and its glorious future:

> Enlarge the place of your tent,
> And let them stretch out the curtains of your dwellings;
> Do not spare; Lengthen your cords,
> And strengthen your stakes.

For you shall expand to the right and to the left,
And your descendants will inherit the nations,
And make the desolate cities inhabited.

                                    —Isaiah 54:2–3 (nkjv)

To "enlarge the place of your tent" means to make room for an increased population. "Your descendants will inherit the nations, and make the desolate cities inhabited" means exactly what it says: Israel will take possession of the nations and develop a barren area into something glorious. This has been the point of God's land grant to Abraham from the very beginning!

Psalm 105:6–11 affirms:

O seed of Abraham His servant,
You children of Jacob, His chosen ones! He is the Lord our
    God;
His judgments are in all the earth. He remembers His
    covenant forever
The word which He commanded, for a thousand
    generations,
The covenant which He made with Abraham, And His oath
    to Isaac,
And confirmed it to Jacob for a statute, To Israel as an
    everlasting covenant,
Saying, "To you I will give the land of Canaan As the
    allotment of your inheritance."

This land grant, which God speaks of repeatedly in the Bible, is more than an ancient curiosity. I believe it is a key to understanding future events—and present responsibilities.

CHAPTER 3
GETTING GOD'S VISION FOR THE LAND GRANT

W E FOLLOWERS OF Christ have an obligation to join with the heavenly host and do our part so that this land grant is realized. I am always surprised when people—Christians, I mean—see an agreement like the one between God and Abraham in the Bible and seem to think it faded away with time or blew away like the dust of an abandoned city. We treat it like a fable. Perhaps some think that God walks away from agreements, or that Abraham's descendants behaved so badly that God abandoned the contract altogether.

No way! First of all, God does not forget. The land grant to Abraham is a mere 4,000 years old. In God's timing, that's yesterday. He looks at us in the 21st century, and Abraham many thousands of years ago, and sees us in the same view. Peter writes that,

> With the Lord a day is like a thousand years, and a thousand years are like a day. The Lord is not slow in keeping his promise, as some understand slowness. Instead he is patient with you, not wanting anyone to perish, but everyone to come to repentance.
> —2 PETER 3:8b–9

Does God abandon His solemn promises? Do His agreements change with each passing generation? Of course not.

Some people I speak with about the land grant are skeptical and point to all the political and cultural barriers that seem to make it unlikely. But I think they have been lulled into complacency. They believe what they see more than what God said.

I'm certain this land grant could be realized—overnight. Let me tell you a true story.

Some time ago there was a rising empire which covered some of the most fertile and abundant land in the world. One day a foreign leader who owned the neighboring territory was under duress because he was fighting a war far away. He offered to sell his territory to this rising empire because he needed money. For a relative pittance he sold the territory, and in an instant the size of the rising empire doubled, without a war or a single loss of life.

This sounds like a fairy tale or something from far-off history. But that rising empire was the United States of America. That transaction was the Louisiana Purchase, the largest—and cheapest—land purchase in our country's history. That territory includes all or parts of 13 states, including Arkansas, Colorado, Iowa, Kansas, Louisiana, Minnesota, Missouri, Montana, Nebraska, North Dakota, Oklahoma, South Dakota, and Wyoming. That foreign leader was Napoleon Bonaparte.

Think of it—we are living on "promised land" ourselves, in this very country! Who's to say this kind of mega-transfer can't happen again, especially when God's promise says that one day, it certainly will?

Let me draw some other parallels between the two situations. When Thomas Jefferson purchased the Louisiana Territory, as it was called, from France, the land was virtually unknown. Aside from New Orleans it was virtually empty of cities, towns or industry. Its only inhabitants were fewer than 100,000 European immigrants and unknown thousands of American Indians who roamed freely over this vast area. That is why Jefferson dispatched Lewis and Clark to explore the newly-acquired territory: to see what was in it. By western standards the land was undeveloped and mostly unutilized in any modern sense. Subsistence living supported a small group of people, but nothing like we see today with the productivity and the development to support hundreds of millions of people.

In the same way today much of the Arab lands included in God's land grant to Abraham are undeveloped or underdeveloped. There are some cities, roads, industry and infrastructure, but nothing like we see in the western world or in Israel itself. There are no capitals of business, industry, arts or technology. Some people live nomadically; many others live in bare subsistence.

Now consider Israel. Anyone who has visited that country comes away amazed at how advanced it is in every way: universities, agriculture, architecture, technology, business and more. It's like a little slice of the U.S. or Europe in the Middle East. One can easily forget, standing on a street corner in Tel Aviv or Jerusalem, that one is not in a major U.S. city. And the Israelis' ability to make much of very little, in everything from farming to high technology, is nothing short of breathtaking.

Now imagine if the land granted to Abraham suddenly came into the possession of Israel. What would happen? Would the transformation be any less than what it was when the U.S. came into possession of that fertile swath of land called the Louisiana Territory, which was larger than Great Britain, Germany, France, Spain, Italy, and Portugal combined?

I personally believe development would happen even more quickly because the technology we have today is unimaginably better than what it was in the early 1800s. I believe we would see a land rush the likes of which the world has never witnessed. Israel would quickly go from its present population of under 10 million to the population of the U.S.—300 million or more. People would flood in, and the kind of development we see in present-day Israel would be extended to the borders of the grant. Israel would in the blink of an eye become the world center of academics, finance, technology, the arts and more.

You think it can't happen? I believe the Bible foretells it. Zechariah 8:20-23 talks about the nations coming to Israel.

> This is what the LORD Almighty says: "Many peoples and the inhabitants of many cities will yet come, and the inhabitants of one city will go to another and say, 'Let us go at once to entreat the LORD and seek the LORD Almighty. I myself am going.' And many peoples and powerful nations will come to Jerusalem to seek the LORD Almighty and to entreat him."

> This is what the Lord Almighty says: "In those days ten
> people from all languages and nations will take firm hold of
> one Jew by the hem of his robe and say, 'Let us go with you,
> because we have heard that God is with you.'"

Many of us are familiar with this passage, but have you ever asked why the nations will come? There must be a reason. I think the reason is obvious: they will come for the commerce, finance, great art and learning, for the temple and the presence of the King. They will come to Israel for many of the same reasons people go to New York or London or Paris today: because these cities are the cultural, financial and political capitals of the world.

That's the kind of vision we need as Christians! We must lift our eyes up and embrace the promise God gave so many years ago to Abraham.

I never saw the movie I'm about to reference, but I heard a line from it that I liked. Bugsy Siegel, the crime boss, went to Las Vegas, looked out over that vast, barren stretch of desert and said, "This is going to be the gambling capital of the world." I like that because it shows vision. That's the kind of vision we Christians need.

As we speed to the end of the age, I believe God is revealing His plan to us in greater detail, drawing our attention to things like his contract with Abraham and the role of Israel in His ultimate plan for the Earth. God's land grant to Abraham obviously conflicts with present-day political boundaries, but which has more integrity, the promise of God or the political boundaries of any given decade? Indeed, the map of the Middle East has been redrawn dozens of times over the recent past, indicating that the plans of men are much more transient than the plans of God.

We need to think big. We need a God-sized vision of what might happen. We need to catch up with what's already happening and learn to recognize the plan of God as it unfolds before our very eyes.

CHAPTER 4
BECOMING PARTNERS WITH GOD

I HAD THE DISTINCT privilege of serving in the U.S. military during the Korean conflict in the 1950s. At one time my unit was under intense fire, pinned down and literally lying flat on the ground to avoid being shot by nearby enemy guns. Our commanding officer had been killed and so we were left to regroup—and pray. I took charge that day. I remembered a psalm I had memorized as a boy, Psalm 91, and all I could do was say it out loud. So I did. In fact, I shouted it, those words ringing against the sound of bullets and artillery flying overhead.

> He that dwelleth in the secret place of the most High shall abide under the shadow of the Almighty.
>
> I will say of the LORD, He is my refuge and my fortress: my God; in him will I trust.
>
> Surely he shall deliver thee from the snare of the fowler, and from the noisome pestilence.
>
> He shall cover thee with his feathers, and under his wings shalt thou trust: his truth shall be thy shield and buckler.
>
> Thou shalt not be afraid for the terror by night; nor for the arrow that flieth by day;
>
> Nor for the pestilence that walketh in darkness; nor for the destruction that wasteth at noonday.
>
> A thousand shall fall at thy side, and ten thousand at thy right hand; but it shall not come nigh thee.
>
> Only with thine eyes shalt thou behold and see the reward of the wicked.

Because thou hast made the LORD, which is my refuge, even the most High, thy habitation;

There shall no evil befall thee, neither shall any plague come nigh thy dwelling.

For he shall give his angels charge over thee, to keep thee in all thy ways.

They shall bear thee up in their hands, lest thou dash thy foot against a stone.

Thou shalt tread upon the lion and adder: the young lion and the dragon shalt thou trample under feet.

Because he hath set his love upon me, therefore will I deliver him: I will set him on high, because he hath known my name.

He shall call upon me, and I will answer him: I will be with him in trouble; I will deliver him, and honour him.

With long life will I satisfy him, and shew him my salvation.

(KING JAMES VERSION)

From that moment on in the battle, not one of our men was lost, although several of us did receive injuries. I was awarded the Purple Heart and the Bronze Star because of my actions that day. I give the credit to God and His power to save. If He had not intervened, we surely would have died.

The reason so many young men went into such dangerous situations with such bravery is that we believed in the mission. While serving in the military I learned that one of the most important types of education a soldier receives is "information education." This is where newly recruited soldiers are told why they are fighting. If you don't know why you are fighting, and don't believe in the goals of the mission, you won't be a good soldier. You will fight halfheartedly. You might turn and run. A man must believe in the cause he is fighting for or he will not give his best effort.

When it comes to the future of Israel and God's land grant to Abraham, Christians need "information education." We need to understand why these things are important to us, why the future of Israel is about more than obscure conflicts taking place half a world away. In a very real sense, God's land grant to Abraham matters to you and me. Why?

Because until it is fully realized, I believe the Lord will not return. Praying for the grant to be fully given will, I believe, speed the coming of the Lord.

What, then, do we do? Is this something we passively wait for, like viewers of some cosmic reality show? No way. The Kingdom of God moves forward by action. Think of the promised land that God gave to the people of Israel. Did He simply hand them the key and let them waltz in, free of struggle or trouble? No. They had to fight for every inch of it. God's promise was that they would be victorious—but they still had to do battle. The book of Joshua chronicles the battles they fought to gain possession of the land already promised to them.

So it is with us. We fight on our knees for God's promises to us, and so we must partner with God and pray with great faith, persistence and energy for this grant to be fulfilled. Imagine if Christians of the western world joined this battle in prayer, pleading with God for Abraham's land to come into Israel's possession. Don't you think it would have an effect? We are promised that the fervent, effectual prayers of the righteous man avail much. Let us avail ourselves of this promise! After all, we have the contract in writing!

And always remember: The sooner the land grant is fulfilled, the sooner this age will come to its fulfillment in Christ.

I recall hearing about prayer groups in World War II who would receive inside information about coming attacks the American forces were about to carry out. They would pray strategically for our armies to win those battles. This is exactly what we see many times in the Old Testament as well, where the strength of Israel's armies depended on the intercession of the people.

Intercessors, now is your time! As Israel is besieged and threatened from all sides we can lend strategic support, upholding their arms even in specific ways. Prayers know no distance. In a very real sense you and I can be on the front lines of this war.

Prayer is far and away the most important thing we can do, but for my part, I'm not content to stop there. I'm a man of action. I like to plan and to build. When I look at the map of the land grant to Abraham, I ask: What could be built there? What is the best way to use and maximize the land? I begin to see how it can be developed and planned like a city or country. Some will be sectioned off for agriculture, some for cities, some made into states and provinces and prepared for habitation. Why can't urban planners and developers look at it now, in advance, so when the time comes it can be developed more speedily? That's the kind of planning God rewards! He is a forward-looking God, and so we can be forward-looking people.

I think again of Lewis and Clark mapping the west on their journey which many called impossible. Their efforts were the first step toward making that vast area productive and liveable. Without them, the Louisiana Territory would have remained a mystery.

I think also of developments closer to home, like the one in my backyard—the City of Irvine. This city of 43 square miles was master-planned down to the square foot before any of it was built. Today it is a model of effective planning, with business centers, parks, universities, and industrial and residential zones laid out in near-perfection. Urban planners come from all over the world to study it. Millions of people are blessed by the foresight that went into this city as they go through their daily lives.

Why did Irvine turn out so well? Because the owners and planners had a vision for what it could become. They not only saw the vision, they put a great deal of energy into planning and developing it—to turn it into a reality.

The same is true of another well-known southern California destination: Disneyland. Walt Disney's original idea was to build a much smaller park in Burbank, California, which was already crowded. Then he enlisted the help of the Stanford Research Institute, an urban planning firm. They scouted a number of possible sites and convinced him to build his park in then-rural Orange County, in a place now called Anaheim. Walt took their advice, caught their vision, and Disneyland is much bigger than it ever would have been had he stuck to his limited vision of building it in Burbank.

That's the kind of vision we need today. That's the kind of planning and foresight we need, too. The land grant to Abraham will be fulfilled just as many other "outrageous" promises to Israel were fulfilled. It is a dependable part of the future. The only question is when it will happen.

I believe the answer is, "Soon."

Join with me and others to provide "air cover" for the nation of Israel. Ask God for the fulfillment of His land grant to Abraham in our own lifetimes even, in the near future. Those who share in the battle share in the spoils. I believe those of us who make this a primary concern will share in the reward when this promise comes to pass.

Let's pray—and work—for it to happen.

Heavenly Father, God of Israel, my hope and trust rest solely in You. Purify my heart and strengthen my faith, as I pray for the people You have chosen as Your own. For Jerusalem, chief of Your joys, I pray for peace and prosperity. From the Mediterranean to the Euphrates, I pray Your people will serve and honor You on every hill, by every road, and out to every border. Let Your will be done and may Your unfolding plans be realized in the land of Israel. While the days of rebuilding draw near, glory to You as You gather the scattered and redeem what is Yours. Amen.

31-DAY PRAYER AND DEVOTIONAL GUIDE

Day 1
Abraham's Promise—and Ours

A NYTHING GOD PROMISED to Abraham is for us, too!
God made promises to Abraham and to all followers of Christ.
We are children of Abraham by faith. In Galatians 2:13–14, Paul
writes that "Christ redeemed us from the curse of the law...so
that in Christ Jesus the blessing of Abraham might come to the
Gentiles." He goes on to say, "And if you are Christ's, then you are
Abraham's offspring, heirs according to promise" (Galatians 2:29).

That verse describes you and me—heirs according to the
promise, and offspring of Abraham by faith!

We share with Abraham so many blessings—our great salvation which is by faith, and the material promise of the land grant.
One day the fulfillment of that promise will bless us personally
even as it blesses the entire world. Paul writes in Romans that "the
promise to Abraham and his offspring that he would be heir of the
world did not come through the law but through the righteousness
of faith." (Romans 4:13) With Abraham, you and I will one day be
heirs of the world, as the Scriptures promise. That's huge!

God's promise to Abraham is also our promise that He will fulfill the specific promises He has given to you and me right now.
God's faithfulness to Abraham should stir up our faith to pray for
the promises he gives us. God's covenant with Abraham gives us
confidence that God will one day accomplish every single thing
He has spoken to us.

It is your right as a child of Abraham and a follower of Christ
to know your future! God told Abraham the future. Jesus said in
John 16:13 that the Holy Spirit would tell us the future, too. God
told the prophet Jeremiah, "Call to me and I will answer you, and
will tell you great and hidden things that you have not known"
(Jeremiah 33:3). If you don't have a promise from God, ask Him
for one. If you do have promises of God, press in and contend for
them in prayer today.

Questions And Meditations

What promises has God given you? Write them down below.

Have you talked to Him about those promises lately? Take a moment now to ask God to fulfill them and to thank Him for them.

Open your ears to anything new God may want to say.

Prayer

Father, thank You for the promises You made to Abraham which You are still fulfilling in our day. Thank You also for the promises You have made to me. I ask in faith that You accomplish them in the right time, in the right way, for Your glory. Amen.

Day 2
Rediscovering God's Plan for Us

IT'S EASY TO forget God's promises to us. At one point the people of Israel literally lost the Scriptures! They were so busy and disconnected from God that they forgot about the Law of Moses and lived however they wanted to live.

Second Kings 22 tells us how Hilkiah, the high priest under King Josiah, rediscovered the book of the law. What was Josiah's reaction? He could have put it on a shelf, or destroyed it or simply ignored it. His response gives us a major key to success in following God:

> "When the king heard the words of the Book of the Law, he tore his clothes."
>
> —2 KINGS 22:11

Josiah repented. Then he called all the elders of Judah to the house of the Lord, read all the words of the Book of the Covenant that had been found in the house of the Lord, and all the people pledged to walk after the Lord with all their hearts and souls.

Wow!

Repentance is the first step in success with God. We remain blind to God's purposes for us if we don't repent of our former ways. If life ever feels directionless or purposeless, that is the signal to get back on track. How? Repent, rediscover, and reconnect with God's promises to you personally and to His people around the world.

One of those promises is God's promise of land to Abraham and by extension to his heirs in the faith. This is a promise many Christians have not heard before and so the situation is much like it was with Josiah: we are hearing it for the first time. What will our reaction be? To obtain the blessing, we must admit that in our ignorance we neglected this great promise.

We can extend that same pattern to our personal lives. Repentance unlocks purpose. It says in the gospel of Luke that,

> "When all the people heard this [Jesus' teaching], and the tax
> collectors too, they declared God just, having been baptized
> with the baptism of John, but the Pharisees and the lawyers
> rejected the purpose of God for themselves, not having been
> baptized by him."
>
> —LUKE 7:29–30

The baptism of John was a baptism of repentance which soft-
ened the hearts of those who accepted it so they would receive
the gospel Jesus preached. But those who hardened their hearts
against repentance "rejected the purpose of God for themselves."
What an amazing truth—and chilling!

Let's be among those who accept the baptism of repentance so
we can clearly see God's purposes in our day.

QUESTIONS AND MEDITATIONS

Have you disregarded or forgotten God's promises to you? Ask for
His forgiveness right now.

In the space below write down the promises you can remember
God has given you. Begin praying over them every morning or
evening—set a time with regularity.

Commit to pray for God's global purposes, especially that the land
grant to Abraham be fulfilled. Our duty as heirs of Abraham is to
co-labor with Christ by contending in prayer for this most precious promise.

Prayer

Lord, forgive me for neglecting or disregarding Your Word and Your promises. I repent and turn to You with a fresh heart and a fresh commitment. Help me to see clearly Your purposes in my life. Help me to partner with Your people around the world in prayer and action. Amen!

Day 3
Connected Faith

D<small>O YOU KNOW</small> that Abraham needs you?

It's true. Hebrews 11 is the famous "hall of faith" chapter in the Bible, listing people like Abraham, Moses, David, and so on. But Hebrews 11:39 tells us something surprising: there is a connection between our faith and the faith of every person listed in the hall of faith. God designed us to need each other! It says,

> "And all these, though commended through their faith, did not receive what was promised, since God had provided something better for us, that apart from us they should not be made perfect."
>
> —H<small>EBREWS</small> 11:39–40

It is staggering to consider that God did not allow these heroes of the faith to receive the promise in their lifetimes because He wanted us all to cross the finish line together—"that apart from us they should not be made perfect." Amazing! And yet that is God's plan.

This tells us that the fight of faith is still being fought, that the promises must still be contended for in prayer and that by our actions today and tomorrow and next week and next year we can stand with the men and women in the hall of faith for the promises they never received. If that doesn't change your life, nothing will!

It is our responsibility as Christians to connect our faith to the promises made to these people, including Abraham. In doing so you literally partner with each of them and will one day share their rewards. Let us pray with urgency for the land grant to be fulfilled and for the many other promises the Bible has for those of us who walk by faith.

QUESTIONS AND MEDITATIONS

Consider for a moment that you and I are part of the fulfillment of promises to Abraham, Moses, and many others. How does that change the way you see your life? Jot your reactions down.

What does it mean to you to "walk by faith"? Share some ideas.

PRAYER

Lord, thank You for the magnificent privilege of part-nering with Your great heroes of the faith! Help me to run my race with the same energy and focus they did, so that when Your promises are fulfilled we can celebrate knowing we did our best, by the grace of God. Amen!

Day 4
Build an Altar of Worship

A BRAHAM WAS NOT just a sojourner, he was a worshiper. Look at his response the first time God mentioned the promise of the land grant:

> "Then the Lord appeared to Abram and said, 'To your descendants I will give this land.' And there he built an altar to the Lord, who had appeared to him. And he moved from there to the mountain east of Bethel, and he pitched his tent with Bethel on the west and Ai on the east; there he built an altar to the Lord and called on the name of the Lord."
>
> —GENESIS 12:7–8

At key points on his journey Abraham worshiped God. Upon receiving the promises he set up altars to commemorate God's visitations. When he returned from Egypt to Canaan, he again called on the name of the Lord (Genesis 13:4). When he moved to Hebron he built an altar there to the Lord (Genesis 13:18). Much later Abraham "planted a tamarisk tree in Beersheba, and there called on the name of the Lord, the Everlasting God" (Genesis 21:33).

Why did Abraham worship when he already had the promise?

Because worship is the only appropriate response to encountering God. The angels and elders around the throne of God constantly fall down before Him crying, "Holy!" For temporary sojourners like us, worship does several things that nothing else can do:

- Worship sustains us on the journey of faith.

- Worship helps us to honor and remember milestones in our journey.

- Worship draws us closer to the God who is worthy of receiving worship.

Hebrews 12:28–29 tells us,

> "Therefore let us be grateful for receiving a kingdom that cannot be shaken, and thus let us offer to God acceptable worship, with reverence and awe, for our God is a consuming fire."

Questions and Meditations:

Do you worship God regularly outside of church? How do you worship Him? Write down some of the ways.

Have you lost a sense of "reverence and awe" for God? What do reverence and awe look like?

How could you offer better worship to God?

_____

_____

_____

_____

_____

_____

_____

_____

_____

_____

_____

Prayer

God of heaven, reveal Yourself to me as a consuming fire. Thank You for a kingdom that cannot be shaken. Help me to offer You acceptable worship, as Abraham did. Amen.

Day 5
Friendship With God

A s we align ourselves with the promise of land to Abraham, we have the privilege of relating to God as Abraham did—as a friend. James 2:23 tells us that Abraham "was called a friend of God."

Wouldn't you like the same to be said of you? Look at the way God related to Abraham throughout his life, on intimate terms as a friend:

- He shared His plans with Abraham. Those plans were to bless Abraham's descendants (Genesis 12:1–3), to destroy the unrighteous cities of Sodom and Gomorrah (Genesis 18:17–19), and his descendants' enslavement and eventual exodus (Genesis 15:13–16).

- He shared a meal with Abraham: "And Abraham ran to the herd and took a calf, tender and good, and gave it to a young man, who prepared it quickly. Then he took curds and milk and the calf that he had prepared, and set it before them [the Lord]. And he stood by them under the tree while they ate" (Genesis 18:7–8).

- He protected Abraham from Abraham's wrong choices (Genesis 20).

- He blessed Abraham's household and businesses. "Now Abram was very rich in livestock, in silver, and in gold" (Genesis 13:2).

God walked with Abraham as a friend—and He will walk with us as friends, too, if we want Him to.

QUESTIONS AND MEDITATIONS:

What qualities of a friend do you value most?

Have you ever felt God's friendship? Describe how.

Let the Holy Spirit bring ideas to mind how you can be a friend of God like Abraham was.

_____

_____

_____

_____

_____

_____

_____

_____

_____

_____

_____

_____

_____

_____

_____

_____

PRAYER

God, I long to be a friend of Yours like Abraham was! Please teach me how to walk with You in friendship. I make this the goal of my life. Amen.

Day 6
God Loves Land

Some people get the idea that God doesn't care about this earth in a physical way, that He is only concerned with spiritual things, that He would never attach any importance to land.

The Bible tells us otherwise. God is often locational. For example, He could have promised to bless Abraham's offspring wherever they went, without tying it to a certain geographical location. He didn't need to promise them actual land. Why not just give them great favor and wealth and influence among all the nations?

Because God loves land, and specific locations play an important part in His plan. Take the mountain slope Jacob deeded to his son Joseph, for instance. Jacob bought this piece of land and erected an altar there which he called "God, the God of Israel." (Genesis 33:20) Later, he gave the slope to Joseph rather than to his older brothers (see Genesis 48:22). Joseph's bones were buried there when he died.

Interestingly, when Jesus had a conversation with a Samaritan woman at the well, it was "near the field that Jacob had given to his son Joseph" (John 4:4). This same piece of property—the actual dirt—figured into accounts of Jacob and of Jesus, hundreds of years apart.

Other examples abound: Jerusalem, of course, and also towns like Bethlehem which God treated as special because it was the home city of David. When the Messiah was to be born, God orchestrated a census that would send Mary and Joseph back to Bethlehem to be registered. Jesus even identified Himself to Saul (Paul) on the road to Damascus as "Jesus of Nazareth."

God is dedicated to geographical areas, perhaps more than we know. It's not just dirt and weeds or buildings to Him; these are places where the goodness of God can flourish. He has a vision for every square inch on the planet. Let's ask for wisdom and

understanding so we can partner with Him in that vision—for the
land grant and every other location on Earth.

Questions and Meditations:

Have you thought about why you live where you live? Have you
ever asked God if you live in the geographical location He wants
you to live in?

Is there any particular property or land you are especially drawn
to? It may be a home, a park, a national park, a vacation spot, or a
type of terrain—beaches, mountains, deserts, forests? Write down
your favorite spots.

Do you believe God has purpose for you in these places? Why and
how?

_____

_____

_____

_____

_____

_____

_____

_____

Prayer

*God, help me to see the value of the land around me
and to catch Your vision and purpose for it. Help me
to know if I am in the right place geographically. I pray
again for the fulfillment of Your promise to Abraham of
land, and for the purpose of all the Earth to be fulfilled
in Your time and in Your way.*

Day 7
Crisis Moments

H AVE YOU EVER been in a crisis where everything seemed lost? I was. My unit and I were pinned down on the battlefront in Korea. Our commanding officer had been killed. My response was to do the only thing I could think of: quote Psalm 91 over and over as enemy bullets streaked overhead. As I lay there shouting that Psalm I felt courage rising within me—supernatural courage. From that moment on we did not lose a man, though several were injured. I believe that God's intervention saved our lives that day.

As challenging as that day was for those of us involved, Abraham faced a more difficult challenge on Mount Moriah. That is where God told him to sacrifice his son Isaac, the son of the promise.

> "When they came to the place of which God had told him, Abraham built the altar there and laid the wood in order and bound Isaac his son and laid him on the altar, on top of the wood. Then Abraham reached out his hand and took the knife to slaughter his son."
> —GENESIS 22:9–10

Can you imagine what was taking place in Abraham's heart? Could you have brought yourself to raise that knife over your own child? Yet if we are to follow Abraham, there will be some extreme tests. Sometimes we will cry out as Jesus did, "My Father, if it be possible, let this cup pass from me" (Matthew 26:39).

God's idea for your life is not that it will be smooth sailing all the way to glory. Jesus personally promised that He would show the apostle Paul "how much he must suffer for the sake of my name" (Acts 9:16). But in those crises we can—and must—choose to believe and obey rather than shrink or turn away.

This goes for God's promise of land to Abraham and our personal lives as well. There will be bumps in the road, full-blown crises and times when it appears that all is lost. But remember the lesson from the battlefront: if we cling to the promised word of the Lord, He will lead us to victory!

Questions and Meditations:

What is the biggest test you have ever been given by God? How did you respond?

What challenges or crises are you facing now? How can you get through them?

_____

_____

_____

_____

_____

_____

_____

_____

_____

_____

_____

_____

Prayer

God, help me through the tests I face right now. Thank You that You want to refine me and take me from glory to glory. Help me to see each crisis as an opportunity to grow closer to You and to advance in Your plan for me here on Earth. Bless Israel and bless my life today.

Day 8
Being Strangers

IF YOU FEEL at home on the earth, something's wrong.
The Bible calls us aliens, sojourners, citizens of another country. This sinful, fallen world is not our home. We should never feel comfortable here.

Abraham is our example in this. God called him out from his father's house and his people, symbolic of us leaving the world. Abraham then wandered for decades in the land of the promise, "yet he [God] gave him no inheritance in it, not even a foot's length" (Acts 7:5). Abraham got good at being a stranger in this world, and so should we.

Paul tells us to "set your minds on things that are above, not on things that are on earth. For you have died, and your life is hidden with Christ in God" (Colossians 3:2–3). Jesus admonished us to lay up for ourselves treasures in heaven, "for where your treasure is, there your heart will be also" (Matthew 6:21).

The key to Abraham's success as a sojourner on Earth was that his eyes were filled with visions of a different kind of city, one whose builder and maker is God.

> "These all died in faith, not having received the things promised, but having seen them and greeted them from afar, and having acknowledged that they were strangers and exiles on the earth. For people who speak thus make it clear that they are seeking a homeland. If they had been thinking of that land from which they had gone out, they would have had opportunity to return. But as it is, they desire a better country, that is, a heavenly one. Therefore God is not ashamed to be called their God, for he has prepared for them a city."
> —HEBREWS 11:13–16

We too can live as those "for whom the world was not worthy" (Hebrews 11:38). Keep your eyes on the ultimate prize.

Questions and Meditations:

How "at home" do you feel in this world, on a scale of 1 to 10 with
1 being "not at home" and 10 being "completely at home"?

How often do you fill your mind with thoughts of the heavenly
city that awaits you? Take a guess, as a percentage, of how much
time you spend thinking of heaven.

What can you do today to stir up in yourself a longing for heaven?
Make a plan to set your affections on things above.

Prayer

*God, give me eyes to see Your heavenly city, and help me
to get my eyes off of temporary things. I commit now to
set my heart on eternal treasures.*

Day 9
The Wandering Aramean

PERHAPS YOUR LINEAGE isn't that great. Some people are descended from pirates, or prisoners, or slaves.

Guess what? It doesn't matter. God made a nation out of a man who was not a nation and who wasn't even called a Jew but rather a "wandering Aramean" (Deuteronomy 26:5). Moses made the people of Israel declare this:

> "And you shall make response before the Lord your God, 'A wandering Aramean was my father. And he went down into Egypt and sojourned there, few in number, and there he became a nation, great, mighty, and populous.'"
>
> —DEUTERONOMY 26:5–6

He was reminding them of their humble heritage and of the great things God did to turn them from nomads into a mighty nation. The prophet Ezekiel spoke for God in even more vivid terms:

> "Thus says the Lord God to Jerusalem: Your origin and your birth are of the land of the Canaanites; your father was an Amorite and your mother a Hittite. And as for your birth, on the day you were born your cord was not cut, nor were you washed with water to cleanse you, nor rubbed with salt, nor wrapped in swaddling cloths. No eye pitied you, to do any of these things to you out of compassion for you, but you were cast out on the open field, for you were abhorred, on the day that you were born.

> "And when I passed by you and saw you wallowing in your blood, I said to you in your blood, 'Live!' I made you flourish like a plant of the field."
>
> —EZEKIEL 16:3–7

Isn't that the story of each one of us? Whose family began high and mighty? Who has only kingly heritage? Not one of us. Therein lies our hope! If God can make a mighty nation out of Abraham's descendants, He can surely do mighty things with you, too. Nothing is too difficult.

In fact, God seems to enjoy using the unlikely people, as Jesus said,

> "I thank you, Father, Lord of heaven and earth, that you have hidden these things from the wise and understanding and revealed them to little children; yes, Father, for such was your gracious will."
>
> —Luke 10:21

Let's not look upon our heritage as limiting God. Rather, let's see through miracle eyes the ways He can use each one of us, as unlikely as we are, to do great things—just like our father in faith, the wandering Aramean.

Questions and Meditations

Have you ever felt held back by your family heritage? How? Why?

What kind of legacy do you want to leave to your children and grandchildren? What are you doing right now to build that legacy?

_____

_____

_____

_____

_____

_____

_____

_____

_____

PRAYER

Lord, before You I am nothing. My past doesn't count. My heritage doesn't matter. Give me the future and the hope You planned for me from long ago. Help me to see that I can do whatever You call me to do—because I am Your child. Amen.

Day 10
Promises by Patience

WAITING FOR GOD to fulfill His promise of land to Abraham can seem to take forever. It's already been more than 3,000 years—how much longer do we have to wait?

Yet waiting is always built into God's plan. Abraham and Sarah had to wait twenty-five years to have a son. Shepherd boy David waited more than twenty years to become king as Samuel had spoken. Jesus waited thirty years to begin His ministry.

We too must wait on our promises—global promises like the grant of land to Abraham, and our personal promises. Hebrews 6:12 tell us we should be "imitators of those who through faith and patience inherit the promises." Faith and patience are a powerful combination. Faith builds in the time of waiting. Jesus commended the churches at Ephesus and Philadelphia for their patient endurance (see Revelation 2 and 3).

When God seems to be taking a long time, remember that the longer something takes to grow, the stronger it will be in the end. He is perfecting His promises for your life even as nothing seems to change.

QUESTIONS AND MEDITATIONS

Have you ever rushed ahead of God and tried to bring a promise to pass by yourself? What was the result?

What are you patiently waiting for now?

_____

_____

_____

_____

_____

_____

_____

_____

_____

_____

_____

_____

_____

_____

_____

_____

_____

_____

_____

_____

_____

_____

_____

_____

PRAYER

Lord, help me to be patient! I am eager for Your promises and sometimes it seems like they are so long in coming. I want to endure these waiting times for You, and for my faith to grow stronger, not weaker, while waiting. Bless Your people, Israel, and remind me today that, though Your promises seem long in coming, they are always worth the wait.

Day 11
Simeon's Promise

SIMEON IS ONE of the most precious and faith-filled men in the Bible and gives us a great example of the patience and faith that can come with waiting.

> "Now there was a man in Jerusalem, whose name was Simeon, and this man was righteous and devout, waiting for the con- solation of Israel, and the Holy Spirit was upon him. And it had been revealed to him by the Holy Spirit that he would not see death before he had seen the Lord's Christ."
>
> —LUKE 2:25–26

One of the only things we know about Simeon is that he was "waiting for the consolation of Israel." Waiting was the key attri- bute of his life! In that time of waiting he established a reputation as "righteous and devout," even among the many other spiritual- minded people in Jerusalem at that time. Talk about faith and patience.

Like Abraham, Simeon seems to have been old by the time of receiving his promise. Upon holding Jesus he said,

> "Lord, now you are letting your servant depart in peace, according to your word; for my eyes have seen your salva- tion that you have prepared in the presence of all peoples."
>
> —LUKE 2:29–31

Simeon's life was ultimately about that one thing, and with that he was ready to go home to be with the Lord.

What is your life about? While waiting for God's promises are you establishing a reputation for righteousness and devotion? Sometimes our promises come toward the end of our life and take a long time to get there. Simeon shows us how to be faithful all the way through.

QUESTIONS AND MEDITATIONS:

Simeon's life was about seeing the Messiah before he died. What one thing is your life about?

Simeon had a reputation for devotion and righteousness. How would your friends describe your reputation?

What would you like to change about your reputation?

PRAYER

Lord, give me the endurance of Simeon, and the ability by Your Spirit to recognize the promise when it comes. Grow me in righteousness and devotion. Help me to walk closely with You and to be sensitive to the leading of Your Spirit as Simeon was. Amen.

Day 12
No Ishmaels

IT CAN BE disastrous to rush the plan of God. As much as we want the land grant to Abraham to happen, imagine seizing the land from hostile nations without God's blessing! No way. It would be wrong and produce a huge mess.

Moses ran into this problem when living in Egypt. It seems that he sensed his calling to lead the people of Israel, and at the age of forty he tried to step into that role. But the time wasn't right. Not only did he go about it the wrong way (by murdering an Egyptian), but his brothers, the Israelites, also rejected his leadership. In fear, Moses fled into the wilderness.

Fear, murder, rejection, disunity—those are the hallmarks of things God is not supporting. And yet forty years later God called Moses to that same task and gave him miraculous success.

At one point Sarah became impatient and encouraged Abraham to have a son by her servant Hagar. That mistake led to heartache later. God helped to redeem that choice, but it was never going to speed up His fulfillment of the promise or change His plan for Isaac. It only complicated matters.

When we try to get results on our own, we produce offspring not of the promise. Human ingenuity or strategy will not cause the land grant promise to be fulfilled. It will be the Spirit of God supporting and leading a willing group of people at the right time and in the right way. Will you be part of it?

QUESTIONS AND MEDITATIONS:

Have you ever tried to seize your promises in the wrong way? What happened as a result?

Do you have evidence of fear, rejection and disunity in any of your efforts now? What might God be telling you?

PRAYER

God, I want to do things Your way. Just as Israel and all Your children look to Your leadership on providing the land grant to Abraham, so I look to You only to lead me in receiving Your promises for my life. Help me not to produce Ishmaels in the meantime. I humble myself before You now.

Day 13
Abraham the Warrior

A BRAHAM WAS MORE than a wealthy guy who walked around the promised land; he was a fearsome warrior.

Maybe you don't recall this less-discussed story about Abraham. After he and Lot separated, Lot began his dubious residency in Sodom and was taken captive during a regional war.

> "When Abram heard that his kinsman had been taken captive, he led forth his trained men, born in his house, 318 of them, and went in pursuit as far as Dan. And he divided his forces against them by night, he and his servants, and defeated them and pursued them to Hobah, north of Damascus. Then he brought back all the possessions, and also brought back his kinsman Lot with his possessions, and the women and the people."
>
> —GENESIS 14:14–16

Notice that Abraham the wanderer possessed a shrewd military mind. He had 318 trained and loyal men standing by for moments like this. He divided his forces, attacked the enemy by night, pressed his advantage in battle and successfully brought back what was stolen. Talk about mopping up the battlefield!

Interestingly, right after Abraham's victory, Melchizedek made his one and only appearance in the Bible. His purpose? To bless Abraham and celebrate with bread and wine!

> "Blessed be Abram by God Most High, Possessor of heaven and earth;
>
> and blessed be God Most High,
>
> who has delivered your enemies into your hand!"
>
> —GENESIS 14:19–20

You and I will be called to fight sometimes while waiting for our promises. Keep in mind that Abraham only went to war once in the biblical record, so we must be careful not to jump into every fight. It must be for a God-appointed purpose—like rescuing family members. When God is in it, He will bless our efforts.

Our job is to prepare, strategize, train, and have courage so when the moment comes we can seize victory. Then God will bless us and exalt His own name as the one "who has delivered your enemies into your hand!"

QUESTIONS AND MEDITATIONS:

What was the most recent battle you feel you fought? Was it a God-appointed battle or one of your own choosing? What was the outcome?

How do you decide if a certain battle is for you to fight or avoid?

What was one of your greatest victories?

PRAYER

Lord, make me brave! Give me the courage and skill of Abraham to lead the fight against enemies of Your purpose. Help me to see which battles are mine to fight, and may Your name be blessed in every victory.

Day 14
Pray With Faith and Fervency

THERE IS ANOTHER kind of battle, and it takes place on our knees. Victorious prayer requires the same fervency that a warrior displays in the midst of battle. Fervency demonstrates love and devotion to our King. Many of us know the verse in James 5:16 that says, "The effective, fervent prayer of a righteous man avails much" (NKJV). Here are three examples of God's love of fervency and passion:

- Mary of Bethany "wasted" a pound of expensive perfume on Jesus' feet. Others thought it wasteful, but Jesus praised her extravagance. In the same way we can extravagantly pray, give, and love, and receive His praise (see John 12).

- King Joash of Israel was commanded to strike the ground with arrows as a symbolic action of his coming victory over Syria. But Elisha the prophet was angry that Joash struck the ground only three times. He said, "You should have struck five or six times; then you would have struck down Syria until you had made an end of it, but now you will strike down Syria only three times" (2 Kings 13:19). Gulp! If Joash had been more fervent in that moment, his victory over Syria would have been much greater.

- Lastly, in the days of Moses, Phinehas bravely ran a spear through an Israelite man who was brazenly sinning with a Moabite woman, and by this action stopped a plague on the people. The Lord made a covenant of peace with Phinehas as a result (see Numbers 25).

God praises those who give Him their very best effort and energy. As we pray, let's do it with gusto!

Questions and Meditations:

How would you describe your "style" of prayer?

Whether loud or soft, do you pray with fervency?

What would give you more passion in prayer? Is it possible you need to reconnect with the promises of God so that the flames of fervency are rekindled?

Prayer

Lord, teach me fervency in all that I do, especially prayer. Help me to pray with the passion You prayed with in the Garden of Gethsemane. Let me never be lukewarm but on fire for Your purposes in my life!

Day 15
Prophetic Significance of the Land Grant

THE SEEDS OF the gospel and of the future of the earth are fore-shadowed in the lives of the patriarchs. We see there glimmers of what God has for us now and what He has in store for humanity in the time to come. For example:

- Abraham's grandson Jacob dreamed of a ladder going to heaven on which angels ascended and descended (see Genesis 28). Jesus later interpreted this dream as referring to Himself (see John 1).

- Isaac was a type of Christ, the promised child born by a miracle. His near-death experience on Mount Moriah foreshadowed the Lamb who would be slain. The ram caught in the thicket symbolized the substitutionary work of Jesus on the Cross (see Genesis 22).

In the same way, God's land grant to Abraham foretells a time when the earth will return to abundance and peace and come under the rule of the King of kings. That is the land you and I will inhabit! It is not simply about enlarging Israel's territory; it's about the very future of the planet and humanity itself.

In that day, Israel will enjoy all the land promised by God to Abraham, while other nations enjoy their own ordained places. But every nation will function under the rule of Jesus who will receive the nations as His special inheritance (see Psalm 2:8-9 and Revelation 11:15).

The land grant is a prophetic message about that soon-coming day when every knee will bow and every tongue confess that Jesus Christ is Lord!

QUESTIONS AND MEDITATIONS:

Do you ever think about what life will be like after Jesus returns? What will you be doing? Where will you live?

What foreshadowing of the gospel do you see in the lives of Abraham and his family? How does this apply to your life now?

PRAYER

Father, give me a bigger view of Your work in history. Help me to see beyond the future I can imagine and into the future You have planned for me as Your child. Tell me more about the prophetic significance of the land grant and other details of the lives of the patriarchs.

Day 16
Mary's Song

WHEN MARY, THE mother of Jesus, rejoiced over the child she was to bring into the world, she linked the promise to the blessing of Abraham:

> "He [the Father] has helped His servant Israel, in remembrance of his mercy, as He spoke to our fathers, to Abraham and to His offspring forever."
>
> —LUKE 1:54–55

Forever! God's promise to Abraham will never end. In His mercy He always remembers it, even to the point of sending His Son to earth. Amazing!

Later in that chapter, Zechariah, father of John the Baptist, tied the coming Messiah to Abraham:

> "…to show the mercy promised to our fathers and to remember His holy covenant, the oath that He swore to our father Abraham, to grant us that we, being delivered from the hand of our enemies, might serve Him without fear, in holiness and righteousness before Him all our days."
>
> —LUKE 1:72–75

God sent His Son out of remembrance of "the mercy promised to our fathers." How enduring the promises to Abraham are! How then will He not fulfill His promise of land to the father of faith?

QUESTIONS AND MEDITATIONS:

Think of a time when God's goodness came into such clear focus that you sang His praises, as Mary and Zechariah did. What would have to happen for you to sing like that again?

Do you have generational promises in your family that you remember together? What are they?

PRAYER

Father, thank You that in Your mercy You remember me. Thank You for being a keeper of promises to all generations, including my ancestors and my children. Help me to praise You and to see Your purposes in what You are doing in my life now, as Mary and Zechariah did. Amen.

Day 17
Right On Time

JESUS' FIRST WORDS in ministry were, "The time is fulfilled" (Mark 1:15). This tells us something about how God works: He has a specific timetable for everything.

This divine timing shows up even in His first covenant with Abraham where He says:

> "Know for certain that your offspring will be sojourners in a land that is not theirs and will be servants there, and they will be afflicted for four hundred years. But I will bring judgment on the nation that they serve, and afterward they shall come out with great possessions. As for you, you shall go to your fathers in peace; you shall be buried in a good old age. And they shall come back here in the fourth generation, for the iniquity of the Amorites is not yet complete."
> —GENESIS 15:13–16

Notice two things. First, He tells Abraham exactly how long his descendants will serve another nation—four hundred years. Then He says one reason for such a long time is that "the iniquity of the Amorites is not yet complete." God even has a timing for His enemies to fill up the measure of their sin.

He also had perfect timing when He sent His Son. Paul wrote,

> "For while we were still weak, at the right time Christ died for the ungodly."
> —ROMANS 5:6

> "But when the fullness of time had come, God sent forth his Son."
> —GALATIANS 4:4

God has perfect timing in your life as well. As you follow Him, His promises will come to pass when they should—not a moment sooner or later.

Questions and Meditations:

Have you ever felt God was late? When?

Do you have a good sense of timing? Can you sing in time, dance in time, tell a good joke, or know when to say the right thing? How does this reflect how God acts?

Prayer

Thank You, Lord, that You plan everything in advance! I trust You with the timing in my life because I see how You have worked throughout history, sending Your Son at just the right time. I know, too, that You will fulfill Your promise to Abraham and to the world of a land grant at just the right time. Even so, do it, Lord Jesus!

Day 18
Suddenly

SOMETIMES THINGS SEEM to take forever. Then suddenly they happen with a swiftness no one could have predicted.

Take the fall of the Soviet Union which seemed to happen overnight after seventy-five years behind the Iron Curtain and communist rule. Or the flood of Noah or the destruction of Sodom and Gomorrah, which caught people completely off-guard. Even the first coming of Jesus took many by surprise; they weren't prepared for it and therefore they did not receive Him.

Complacency is the great enemy of passion and preparedness. Jesus sternly warned every human being:

> "But concerning that day or that hour, no one knows, not even the angels in heaven, nor the Son, but only the Father. Be on guard, keep awake. For you do not know when the time will come…And what I say to you I say to all: Stay awake."
> —MARK 13:32–33, 37

As we wait and pray for the land grant to be fulfilled, along with our own personal promises, let's not become complacent. Stoke the fire of expectation in your heart morning by morning because one day the promise will be completed—and perhaps suddenly.

QUESTIONS AND MEDITATIONS:

Have you ever had something happen very suddenly that you were not expecting? What happened? Was it good or bad?

How do you renew your passion for the Lord on a daily basis? What works for you to keep the fire burning bright?

PRAYER

Lord, forgive me for ever losing my passion for You and for not being ready at all times for Your promises to come to pass. I want to be like an expectant bride waiting for Your return. As I stoke the fire again, let Your Holy Spirit blow on the embers of my heart.

Day 19
All Nations Will Be Blessed

ABRAHAM'S LAND GRANT isn't just about Israel. It's about Israel becoming a light to all nations.

That is what God originally intended. Indeed, His promise to Abraham was that "in you all the families of the earth shall be blessed" (Genesis 12:3b). Wow! That's a big promise, and not just for one group but for every ethnicity and tribe and nation on earth.

The prophets repeated this promise, as in Isaiah:

> "The nations will come to the brightness of your rising."
> —Isaiah 60:3

Even Jesus rebuked Israel for not being a "city on a hill" as God intended (Matthew 5:14). That city was supposed to spread the knowledge of God over the whole Earth.

Praying for God to bless Israel is to pray for God to bless the world, including all Gentile nations. As God promised to Abraham, "I will bless those who bless you, and him who dishonors you I will curse" (Genesis 12:3a). James, the brother of Jesus and a pillar of the church in Jerusalem, quoted the Lord speaking through the prophet Amos:

> "After this I will return, and I will rebuild the tent of David that has fallen; I will rebuild its ruins, and I will restore it, that the remnant of mankind may seek the Lord, and all the Gentiles who are called by my name, says the Lord, who makes these things known from of old."
> —Acts 15:16–18

Let's pray for Israel so the entire world will be blessed!

QUESTIONS AND MEDITATIONS:

Have you ever prayed for Israel? Do you find it difficult or easy?

How can you be a "city on a hill" right where you live and work? Make some notes on how.

PRAYER

Lord, help me to reflect the light of Your glory just as Israel reflects the light of Your glory for all nations. Make me a shining lamp, a city on a hill whose light draws others to You. And help Israel to rise to its calling, shining forth the knowledge and glory of Your Son over all the Earth.

Day 20
One New Man

THE GOSPEL OF Jesus Christ does more than unite Jew and Gentile in a common faith. In Christ we will actually become "one new man in place of the two" as Ephesians 2:15 says. This is an amazing and mysterious reality. Paul confirms this elsewhere saying that in Christ there is neither Jew nor Greek (Galatians 3:28).

This means there are no second-class citizens. We are all children of Abraham by faith—no stepchildren. Blood may be thicker than water, but to be a child of God trumps them both! In Him we all are a new creation:

> "From now on, therefore, we regard no one according to the flesh. Even though we once regarded Christ according to the flesh, we regard him thus no longer. Therefore, if anyone is in Christ, he is a new creation. The old has passed away; behold, the new has come."
> —2 CORINTHIANS 5:16–17

And,

> "For not all who are descended from Israel belong to Israel, and not all are children of Abraham because they are his offspring, but 'Through Isaac shall your offspring be named.' This means that it is not the children of the flesh who are the children of God, but the children of the promise are counted as offspring."
> —ROMANS 9:6–8

It's almost as if, having started with one man, Adam, God is culminating human history by bringing all people back into unity. The destiny of all nations is not just linked in partnership; it is the same! For us, and for every believer, that means having confidence as full sons and daughters, inheritors of the promises to Abraham. Some day we will experience what it means to be "one new man" in an even fuller and more glorious way. Let's pray as Peter exhorted us, to "speed His coming" (2 Peter 3:12). Amen!

Questions and Meditations:

Are you part of an easily identifiable ethnic group? How big a part does that culture play in your life?

How does it feel to you to be a new creation in Christ? Describe your feelings briefly below.

Prayer

Father, thank You for having a big family with lots of children. Help me to embrace my brothers and sisters in Christ today and to see them as You see them: as new creations in You. May we come to the unity You desire— and may You come quickly. Amen!

Day 21
God Loves Jerusalem

D ID YOU KNOW that God has a favorite city? It's not New York or Paris or Tokyo or Moscow, as beautiful and interesting as those cities are. The Bible makes clear that God loves Jerusalem. No other city in the Bible receives His passionate attention. Consider God's own words:

> "Thus says the Lord of hosts: I am jealous for Zion with great jealousy, and I am jealous for her with great wrath. Thus says the Lord: I have returned to Zion and will dwell in the midst of Jerusalem, and Jerusalem shall be called the faithful city, and the mountain of the Lord of hosts, the holy mountain."
> —ZECHARIAH 8:2–3

> "Jerusalem shall be called the throne of the Lord, and all nations shall gather to it"
> —JEREMIAH 3:17

Jesus called Jerusalem "the city of the great king" (Matthew 5:35) and lamented,

> "O Jerusalem, Jerusalem, the city that kills the prophets and stones those who are sent to it! How often would I have gathered your children together as a hen gathers her brood under her wings, and you were not willing!"
> —LUKE 13:34

But that's not the end of the story. He promises to return:

> "I tell you [Jerusalem], you will not see me until you say, 'Blessed is he who comes in the name of the Lord!'"
> —LUKE 13:35

There will come a day when Jesus returns and Jerusalem blesses Him! Not only that but He will rule from Jerusalem and His throne will be there (see Revelation 22:3). Let's commit to understand God's heart for Jerusalem, which will be the capital not only of the enlarged Israel promised to Abraham, but of the whole Earth.

QUESTIONS AND MEDITATIONS:

Have you ever prayed for the peace of Jerusalem as the Bible commands? (See Psalm 122:6) Have you ever visited Jerusalem in person?

Consider the following scriptures:

- Ezekiel 5
- Psalms 48, 122, 132
- Isaiah 2, 60, 62, 66

In light of these, how would you describe God's heart toward Jerusalem?

PRAYER

Lord, give me a burning passion for the city of Jerusalem and its purpose just as You have. Help me to see how it fits into Your plan for my life and for the world. Thank You for this city and for how You continue to use it in history to bless the nations. I pray for the peace of Jerusalem today. Amen.

Day 22
Take It Slow

God did not bring the children of Israel into the promised land all at once. They couldn't have handled it. God said,

> "I will not drive them [your enemies] out from before you in one year, lest the land become desolate and the wild beasts multiply against you. Little by little I will drive them out from before you, until you have increased and possess the land."
> —Exodus 23:29–30

Imagine getting everything God has promised you in one instant. It sounds great, but the truth is you would probably fall apart! It's not easy to sustain new blessings or handle the troubles that come with great blessing. Entering your promised land is a battle, not a cake walk. Anyone who thinks they can waltz into the promises of God without opposition clearly has not read the Bible's account of Joshua leading the people of Israel into their promised land. It's full of fighting, bravery, death, and difficulty—and ultimately great victory.

Let's be thankful that God is willing to take us there slowly. Yes, there will be "suddenlies" in our lives when blessings come overnight, but more often He will gently lead us forward at a pace we can handle. This will build our strength and wisdom so we can confidently occupy our land of promise for a long time to come.

Questions and Meditations:

What are some examples of God moving slowly and deliberately in your life?

Have you ever experienced a blessing that also brought trouble? Explain.

Prayer

Lord, thank You for Your kindness and gentleness in leading me into my destiny. I want to honor You with my courage and zeal, but also with patience and a teachable spirit. Bless me now as You bless Israel, and may we enter our promises on Your schedule and in Your strength.

Day 23
Keep Driving Out the Enemy

As valiant and successful as he was, Joshua made a big mistake: he did not drive out all the nations God told him to.

> "Now Joshua was old and advanced in years, and the Lord said to him, 'You are old and advanced in years, and there remains yet very much land to possess.'"
> —Joshua 13:1

> "Yet the people of Israel did not drive out the Geshurites or the Maacathites, but Geshur and Maacath dwell in the midst of Israel to this day."
> —Joshua 13:13

> "…they did not drive out the Canaanites who lived in Gezer, so the Canaanites have lived in the midst of Ephraim to this day but have been made to do forced labor."
> —Joshua 16:10

That failure haunted the people for centuries to follow.

Have you stopped part-way in taking your promised land, too? Are there things you are tolerating in your life that God clearly wants to remove? If you haven't discovered it by now, God is gentle but also relentless. He is like a refiner's fire and He will not stop purifying us until we are holy as He is holy.

The establishment of Abraham's land grant may take relentless energy, too. Rather than happening overnight it may take years or decades to possess and establish it. Let's be prepared to stick with the task to the very end. In the same way let's never give up the battle against "foreign enemies" in our own lives, those thoughts and habits that drive us from God.

Questions and Meditations:

Is there anything in your life that you know God is asking you to stop doing—or start doing?

Talk about a time when you tolerated something that came back to haunt you.

Prayer

Lord of heaven's armies, give me Your zeal for holiness. I am listening; point out things I need to drive out of my life starting today. I ask Your forgiveness for allowing enemy thoughts and habits to reside in my heart. Amen.

Day 24
Rescue Your Loved Ones

A BRAHAM EMBODIES A very special aspect of God's heart: the commitment to rescue loved ones from disaster.

We saw how Abraham demonstrated God's heart by rescuing his nephew Lot when Lot and his family were captured in a war (see Genesis 14). Later, Abraham pleaded with God for Sodom and Gomorrah to be spared, probably on account of Lot and his family (see Genesis 18).

God was willing to listen to Abraham because Abraham reflected God's very heart. He is the Shepherd who leaves the flock to save the sheep that wandered off. He is the God who sent His Son on a rescue mission for all humanity, to save us from hell. Jesus said, "the Son of Man came to seek and to save the lost" (Luke 19:10).

In the same way we should intercede for the land of Israel, and for our loved ones. Proverbs 11:30 tells us that "whoever captures souls is wise." What a great picture! The word "capture" brings to mind forcibly taking someone away from danger, like a soldier dragging a wounded man to safety, or like the angels literally seizing Lot and his family and compelling them to leave Sodom (see Genesis 19).

If you're not in the rescue business, get into it now. Plead with God for the peace of Israel and for the well-being of those in your earthly and spiritual families. Then you will be like father Abraham, reflecting the heart of Father God.

QUESTIONS AND MEDITATIONS:

Have you ever rescued someone from danger? How?

Have you ever been rescued from danger? How did you feel toward your rescuer?

What can you do now to go after lost sheep and people in spiritual danger? Make a plan below.

PRAYER

Good Shepherd, give me Your heart for people. Only love would drive someone into harm's way for the sake of another. Help me to be like Your Son who showed the greatest love by laying down his life for his friends. Help me to lay down my life for Your people, for Israel, and for my loved ones. Amen.

Day 25
Keep the Main Thing the Main Thing

ABRAHAM HAD A lot of options. He had become wealthy and powerful. He could live where he wanted to, buy whatever he wanted, make alliances with powerful kings, even find a daughter for his son Isaac from among kings in the surrounding nations. Abraham was in a great position to be a regional power broker, and intermarriage was a big part of that (see Genesis 34).

But in the midst of his plenty, Abraham was not seduced by power. He kept his eyes on one thing: the promise God had given him of a great nation. That's why he made his servant swear "you will not take a wife for my son from the daughters of the Canaanites, among whom I dwell, but will go to my country and to my kindred, and take a wife for my son Isaac" (Genesis 24:3b–4).

This seemingly simple decision honored God greatly. Abraham was again putting his trust entirely in God with the most important thing in his life: his own descendants through Isaac.

We too must not be distracted or tempted to treat our promises like common things. Like the writer of Hebrews we should,

> "lay aside every weight, and sin which clings so closely, and let us run with endurance the race that is set before us."
> —HEBREWS 12:1

Jesus told about people who would be made unfruitful because of riches and cares:

> "As for what was sown among thorns, this is the one who hears the word, but the cares of the world and the deceitfulness of riches choke the word, and it proves unfruitful."
> —MATTHEW 13:22

Abraham is a great example of how to finish strong, to not be distracted by the opportunities for power and influence and wealth the world gives us, but to keep our eyes locked in on the promise God has for us.

QUESTIONS AND MEDITATIONS:

What are some of the most distracting things in your life? List a few.

How do you stay focused on the promises rather than other possibilities life throws your way?

PRAYER

Lord, even as You bless me I will not take my eyes off the promises and tasks You have given me. I will turn neither to the left nor right but, like Abraham at the end of his life, will drive toward the high calling You have given me in Christ Jesus. I pray today for the fulfillment of all Your promises to Abraham, and I look forward to being part of those promises as a child of Yours. Amen.

Day 26
Receive Glory to Give Glory

D o you realize that we were made for glory? God created people and nations and the planet to possess and reflect His glory. Paul wrote that,

> "There are heavenly bodies and earthly bodies, but the glory of the heavenly is of one kind, and the glory of the earthly is of another. There is one glory of the sun, and another glory of the moon, and another glory of the stars; for star differs from star in glory."
>
> —1 Corinthians 15:40–41

One day you and I will be "raised in glory" (v. 43).

> "And we all, with unveiled face, beholding the glory of the Lord, are being transformed into the same image from one degree of glory to another. For this comes from the Lord who is the Spirit."
>
> —2 Corinthians 3:18

Why does God give us glory? So we can give it back to Him! In the age to come,

> "the kings of the earth will bring their glory into it [the New Jerusalem]…They will bring into it the glory and the honor of the nations."
>
> —Revelation 21:24, 26

Get ready—God is training us to bear His glory so that we can reflect Him in ever-greater measure. When God fulfills the promise of land to Abraham, it will be glorious and will abound to God's glory. When God gives you a promise and fulfills it in your life, He gets glory for it!

It's an amazing reality that He wants us to partake in His glory.

We can only give glory that we have first received. Let's press into that glory, beholding Him with an unveiled face.

Questions and Meditations:

Have you ever experienced a special manifestation of the glory of God? What was it like? How did it change you?

What do you imagine the glory of God looking like? Feeling like?

Do you ever pray for God's glory to be revealed in you? Now's a good time to start!

Prayer

Father, I cry as Moses did—show me Your glory! Let me behold You with an unveiled face. Send me Your Spirit in greater measure than ever before, and train me to be a vessel of honor so that through my life You will receive glory and honor and praise forever.

Day 27
Abraham Is Cheering for You

W E TEND TO think that Abraham is some long-lost figure obscured by the mists of time. But Jesus assured us that Abraham is very much alive, as indeed all are alive to God (see Luke 20:38).

In fact, Hebrews 12:1 tells us where Abraham is: among the great cloud of witnesses. It says we are "surrounded" by this cloud of witnesses, implying that they see all that we do and are rooting for us to succeed. Can you picture Abraham watching you go through your day? How about your own loved ones who have gone on to be with the Lord? What would make them proud of you today?

This passage in Hebrews encourages us in light of that cloud of witnesses to run our race with endurance. God has set before each of us a race, a particular course. No two are alike, but the same thing is required from each of us: endurance.

Let's borrow from the attitude of Jesus "who for the joy that was set before Him endured the cross, despising the shame, and is seated at the right hand of the throne of God. Consider Him who endured from sinners such hostility against Himself, so that you may not grow weary or fainthearted" (Hebrews 12:2–3).

QUESTIONS AND MEDITATIONS:

How do you feel when you consider that you are surrounded by a great cloud of witnesses?

When you grow weary, how do you normally respond? Is there a better response?

Are you able to have joy when enduring the hardest parts of life? What's one circumstance where you succeeded in being joyful even in the face of hostility or unfair treatment?

Prayer

Jesus, You gave us the perfect example of enduring. Thank You for the cloud of witnesses who by their example encourage me to run my course with endurance and faithfulness. Help me today to do what You have given me to do so that I may be counted among the faithful. Amen!

Day 28
Together in One Accord

PRAYING ALONE IS wonderful. Jesus often went off alone to pray. But there is a particular power when we pray together. It was during a prayer meeting that the Holy Spirit baptized the first believers:

> "All these with one accord were devoting themselves to prayer."
>
> —ACTS 1:14

> "And suddenly there came from heaven a sound like a mighty rushing wind, and it filled the entire house where they were sitting. And divided tongues as of fire appeared to them and rested on each one of them. And they were all filled with the Holy Spirit and began to speak in other tongues as the Spirit gave them utterance."
>
> —ACTS 2:2–4

> "Later they prayed again, 'And when they had prayed, the place in which they were gathered together was shaken, and they were all filled with the Holy Spirit and continued to speak the word of God with boldness.'"
>
> —ACTS 4:31

That's the kind of prayer we want! As we pray for God to fulfill His promised land grant to Abraham, and as we lift up our own lives to Him, we want prayers that reach heaven and invite a powerful response. Let's make it a top priority to find groups of believers with whom we can pray for Israel, as well as offering up personal requests and prayers for our churches and the body of believers.

What's more important than connecting with God in prayer? Nothing!

QUESTIONS AND MEDITATIONS:

Who do you know who really believes in prayer?

What are your habits of prayer? How often do you pray? Where? When?

What can you do starting today to pray more effectively? Write some ideas.

PRAYER

Lord, prayer is the first step in any good work. I pray now for the promises to Israel and Abraham to be fulfilled. I pray with my many brothers and sisters who are praying for the same thing around the world. Help us to join together in communities of prayer so that with one accord we can devote ourselves to prayer as the early church did. Amen.

Day 29
Sarah's Faith

ABRAHAM STANDS so tall in Bible history that it's easy to overlook his wife Sarah, who arguably had more faith than Abraham did sometimes! Hebrews 11:11–12 tells us,

> "By faith Sarah herself received power to conceive, even when she was past the age, since she considered him faithful who had promised. Therefore from one man, and him as good as dead, were born descendants as many as the stars of heaven and as many as the innumerable grains of sand by the seashore."

Clearly, Sarah's faith combined with Abraham's faith made the promise possible. Paul even made Sarah an example of the freedom we have in Christ, saying,

> "So, brothers, we are not children of the slave but of the free woman [Sarah]."
>
> —GALATIANS 4:31

We are not just sons and daughters of Abraham, we are sons and daughters of Sarah! It probably took a lot more faith for Sarah to believe that she would conceive in old age than that Abraham could have children in old age, just for the physical fact that men can produce children into old age while women stop conceiving much earlier. Who knows what was going on in Sarah's mind as Abraham kept reminding her of God's promise that she would conceive? No wonder on at least one occasion she laughed! (See Genesis 18:12.)

But ultimately Sarah's faith is a rock on which we can all stand because it is faith in God who brings even impossible promises to pass.

QUESTIONS AND MEDITATIONS:

Have you ever held onto a promise that just seemed impossible? What kept your faith steady?

Have you witnessed a physical miracle? Explain.

How did this boost your faith and the faith of those who heard about it?

PRAYER

God, give us the faith of Sarah. She believed not just God but Abraham who heard from God about the promise. May we live in the freedom she represents, and may the promises to her offspring of land and blessings be fulfilled speedily.

Day 30
Look to the Future

ABRAHAM WAS FUTURE-ORIENTED. How do we know? He made detailed negotiations for his own burial place. Indeed, an entire chapter of the Bible is given to the account of Abraham buying a burial place for himself, Sarah and their ancestors (see Genesis 23). That purchase would bless his family for generations to come.

His planning for the future blessed his heirs. Jacob, Abraham's grandson, later said,

> "Soon I will die and join my ancestors. Bury me with my father and grandfather in the cave in the field of Ephron the Hittite. This is the cave in the field of Machpelah, near Mamre in Canaan, that Abraham bought from Ephron the Hittite as a permanent burial site. There Abraham and his wife Sarah are buried. There Isaac and his wife, Rebekah, are buried. And there I buried Leah. It is the plot of land and the cave that my grandfather Abraham bought from the Hittites."
> —Genesis 49:29–32, NLT

Abraham's foresight shaped his family legacy. It gave his children, grandchildren, and great-grandchildren a sense of place, of belonging, of history.

And his ancestors inherited much more than a burial place; they inherited a vision. A vision of God granting to them not a single burial cave but an entire nation with borders stretching beyond where the eye could see or the mind could dream. Their bones were buried in the cave near Mamre by faith that one day Abraham's vision of a land grant would come true.

And it will!

QUESTIONS AND MEDITATIONS:

What vision are your children and grandchildren inheriting from you?

What practical plans have you put in place to promote that vision when you are gone?

How are you shaping your family legacy in other ways?

PRAYER

Lord, give me a vision for my future! Help me to use my money and skills and influence to build a legacy worth living and hand off that vision to my children. Amen.

Day 31
Never Stop Praying

A BRAHAM GIVES US an example of faithfulness and belief over a period of decades in a promise that must have seemed impossible, delayed and uncertain. He had no Bible to rely on for comfort and inspiration. He did not possess the indwelling Holy Spirit. He had only his relationship with the living God to guide him.

And yet he never stopped.

That is the example we must follow. Paul exhorted us in one of his letters to "never stop praying" (1 Thessalonians 5:17, New Living Translation). That is the goal of this prayer guide: to encourage you to never stop praying for the promises to Abraham to come to pass in their entirety, and to give you inspiration to pray for your personal promises as well.

We have looked at many examples of God's faithfulness in these weeks and have heard the sure word that our God will do all that He says He will do. Let's "press on toward the goal for the prize of the upward call of God in Christ Jesus" (Philippians 3:14).

Never stop praying. For God's land grant to Abraham. For Israel. For your life and calling. For your family. For your children. For God's kingdom to come and His will to be done.

Never stop praying!

QUESTIONS AND MEDITATIONS:

What are some habits and commitments you can make right now to help you pray consistently?

Think of a time when you prayed regularly and passionately. What motivated you then?

Stir up those same motivations now. Return to your first love and pray with passion!

_____

PRAYER

*God, I commit to pray often and with an open and pas-
sionate heart about Israel and the world, and about my
own situation. I pray for my church, my family, my neigh-
borhood, my job, and my future. Bless me with Your presence as I seek You, Lord. May Your will be done in Israel
and around the world as it is in heaven. Amen!*

"So [it shall be] that he who invokes a blessing on himself in the land shall do so by saying, may the god of truth and fidelity [the amen] bless me; and he who takes an oath in the land shall swear by the god of truth and faithfulness to his promises [the amen], because the former troubles are forgotten and because they are hidden from my eyes."

—Isaiah 65:16